Living Next Door
To The City

Living Next Door To The City

ELAINE EVELEIGH

To order additional copies of this book, contact:
Xlibris
800-056-3182
www.Xlibrispublishing.co.uk
Orders@Xlibrispublishing.co.uk
745297

CONTENTS

BROKEN

A herring gull with a broken wing
a stubborn sinew still secures
drags it over the arranged stones.
Moving with difficulty, an old woman
with too much shopping,
she can't manage, can't abandon.
Such an encumbrance
but he's going to be lost without it.

On the beach he finds his sea legs.
Almost struts towards the shore
gull gait more faithful than feathers.
Trying to ignore the lopsidedness,
an old trooper coming on to sing
as though, looks and voice and fans
hadn't deserted him. Yesterday's mates
fly up above, secure in wings efficiency.
Looking down, but not at him,
complex eye, cherry picking tide's bounty.

So at home up there, so familiar,
model bird shapes white on blue.
Saying summer on our photographs.
So many good fairies at their christening,
their birthright to inherit, land, sea, and sky.
Follow the boat, the plough and street party.

The disabled seagull pecks at sand.
How long before his body lies
swollen in waves swell?

Life's a beach and then....

A VIEW FROM CHILDHOOD

It looked like bravado
That confidence made of skill and experience.
Snipping through silk, independent
of draughts or scissors approach.
A life of its own.

Expensive wool coating reduced to a cut out toy.
Turquoise brocade brought back from Thailand.
'You could have got the same thing
in Brights last year,' sniffs my mother.

But she is only the seamstress.
The little woman up the hill,
the cutter and shaper, eventual creator.
Who is she to destroy illusions. Exclusive
to them, this bolt from the blue.
Long haul holiday justified.

Awkward women who want to look
like the slim Siamese girls.
Faults of middle age and sturdy genetics
forgiven, hidden, with bias and folds.
'A bit down on the shoulder'
'A bit up on the sides'
Magazines make promises
Real bodies decide.

Eager as the young brides
Figures hugged in white, obvious as X rays,
or teenagers pruning their jeans,
all in at the seams. School dresses
for me and my sister. Mine yellow check,
hers, square necked, plain green.

The pedestrian needs of trousers with failed zips,
pockets that leaked money and secrets
when clothes were made and mended
not sharing a trolley with groceries in Sainsbury's
picked over in aid of Oxfam and Hospices.
Keyed in at any old time.

Always the sewing machine, vibrating,
making sense of material dreams
Till all satisfied, paraded,
the catwalk of our cold front room.

CUT FLOWERS

The magenta anemones
are dying, they're doing it in style.
Stems twisting towards the light,
petals stretched as if, cosmetic surgery
had been involved.
'Don't give in to time, call,
Flora Solutions 212415.'

No longer obedient, who sprang up so eagerly,
attention seeking teenagers displaying all their wares.
Now grope in arthritic trauma
or flabbier stem discovers
its bend is permanent, leans
awkwardly on fellow flower, sags,
against the rim of the vase
needing so much support.

The leaves have forgotten their greenness.
The natural curliness of youth
crimped into senility, anticipate,
the slow compost.
As for the dark centres,
their coquetry turns to desperation
sprinkling black dust onto table's litter,
their disaffection contagious as a sneeze.

This is the death bed scene,
petals darken at the edges
thin out like teeth in diseased gums.
Draw in on themselves, lose
interest in those with whom they
shared same stamen. Till,
the first one falls, staining the carpet.
Alarming as blood.

BIBURY CHURCHYARD

Sometimes on a summer afternoon
Pub lunch eaten. Beauty spot's
claim to fame exploited.
The Abbey shop and museum already visited
seek the shade of Yews in a quiet churchyard.
feel some empathy with
the Sarah's and Elizabeth's who departed
long before I came, yet for the most part
outlived, their Johns and Williams.

The years between the lives,
the discrepancy so wide.
How could they be reunited?
In human terms the gap not close
a toothless old Elizabeth, joined
with John, still in his prime?

From my perspective, pink standard roses
bordering the path, grey stones remark
the sadness of their losses, wife and mother
much loved husband, infant son,
their grief all one.

Old bones at home here
beneath the stones and roses
as swallows make the sky their own.

IN THE BLEAK MIDWINTER

Christmas day, a white one at last.
How I dreamed along with Bing,
of white Christmases. Well beyond
my childhood, the excitement of seeing it fall
the dark world behind the evening curtains,
snow turning on the light.
Changing everything,
swirling snowflakes painting the garden,
making beggars of the birds and pioneers
of neighbours retrieving their paths.
Now our hill's been gritted,
only the parked cars, sleeping statues,
being rudely woken by shovelling figures.

Snow stays around in this cold December
its inconveniences highlighted on newsreels
that concentrate on airports, frozen planes.
Escape routes blocked
relatives separated by air miles.
Going Home for Christmas more than a winter hike.
We who stay put, can appreciate each tree iced,
each rubbish bin, hidden, differences obliterated.

On Christmas day while turkeys'
flabby carcass times itself with an inserted clock
knows exactly when flesh turns to meat
walk up to the Pub, a Pub
I've known my whole life through.
Here I came to buy my mothers cigarettes,
younger than I am now
when she died of lung cancer.

I feel too old for Christmas but
the occasion fills the Miners Rest.
Mostly strangers, people who come from
the new houses, friends when ways be foul
and the Christian calendar demands
we celebrate the birth of a baby boy
few of us believe was significant.
Still hang a bauble on our ancestors beliefs,
pick holly, send cards, deck trees
the streets a festival of light.

Outside, among the smokers, who are first in line
there's a rumour going round that a body
has been found in Longwood lane.
Just up the road from us, where we walk the dog,
cross the road to go through 'Heidi's wood.'
Heidi wrote her name on the smooth bark
of that beech when she was a schoolgirl, it still stands,
the tree, the tidy signature. Heidi was murdered
by her husband when she was twenty one.
Not realizing she'd carved, her own memorial.

Now this new horror spills, over Christmas day.
We've all heard about the missing woman,
seen her photograph on television,
fair-haired, good face, wide smile
last seen at The Ram, a Pub I've drank in
where the wine is pricey and the customers are young.
There's live music on a Thursday.

Joanna, twenty five, lived in a Clifton flat,
not far away as crows fly
and cars cross the suspension bridge.
Now too close to home.
The anguish of her parents
her brother and her boyfriend
for whom this event, will run and run
regardless of seasons and weather
as a landscape architect becomes
a part of our landscape, a part
of this Christmas, woven in.

Police erect those ominous little tents
beloved of murder mysteries. Search for clues.
Later they'll ask for an odd grey sock and a Pizza box
the debris of Jo's last hours becoming evidence.

Christmas closes quickly, by new year
we're all in fancy dress.
'I found her,' says Dan, a man in a cowboy hat,
'but keep it stum,' as he tells everyone.

There's no new year for Jo
Fresh cut flowers lean against the quarry wall
while at the crossroads a dead bouquet
still attached to the signpost, for a young man
Jack, killed in a traffic accident, who
I only know through photographs, of him in a gym,
playing games, pinned regularly
to this, his finishing post.

Down the Coombe, where a small yew tree
interrupts the beeches on the bend,
guards a stone naming two teenagers.
"Joyrider's" the papers said, not much joy is left
so much they've missed
since that unlicensed drive.

Tragedies merge, a flock of pigeon's
fly up from beech mast
where earlier last year I picked up
a dead blue tit, weighing nothing in my hand.

SHELLED

Coming home from the Pub on a wet night
I kick a snail aside
to save it from the awful crunch
as husband or son
steps down its thin defences
ends its slimy hold, on leaf
and life and garden path.

Though not expecting snail to understand
righting itself slowly among the penstamens
probably complains to fellow gastropods.
"Had a bloody time of it last night
one of those bigfoots kicked me,
viscous bastard nearly cracked the roof."
"You were on the path?"
"I was trying to get to the greenside."
"Asking for it, you know its dangerous,
I don't go there anymore,
big brownie bought it, yellowshell and whirly"
"OK, OK, I know the risks
but they're so full of spite."
"It could be worse, they put
the blue stuff down next door."
"The blue stuff, I'm not into that
it's lethal, criminal, a massacre."
"Can't keep the kids off it though
turned a generation into addicts."

"Got the T shirt;
"Save the Hostas; Cost us."
"I had an ancestor who got eaten
by a man. He was a hundred."
"What the man?"
"No great, great granddad, a brown shell
with exceptional markings.
well so they said. Perhaps its just apocryphal?"
"It might be true, tramps used to pick the walls
up there when there were cottages
and people still grew cabbages
before the new estate, those silly fences
shiny tiles and foreign plants"
"We have a history of persecution.
Still if it rains I'll try again tonight,
some do get across the path."
"Some do. You're right.
But there's no greenside.
That's the myth."

CONCORDE

A long nosed triangle cutting through sky and time
It became a familiar sight, its particular sound
significant as church bells
our local god reminding us to look up.

After today, never again.
Our cameras wave goodbye
Picture it, roaring over the suspension bridge'

Another famous Bristol icon,
Moving people from place to place
Clifton to Abbotsleigh, just
one river to cross.

Maybe Concorde went too fast,
we weren't in that much of a hurry.
Burnt itself out, a bridge has more staying power.

Plane moves on to greet the crowds
At Clevedon, Portishead, Cumberland Basin
One last look at the Downs,
to land eventually in Filton.
Going home on a wing and a dare.

CONSIDERING LILIES

She planted lilies and was full of hope.
Taking each bulb from its mousy nest
to bury in the sticky soil.
And, as one does, imagined,
a summer night with lilies glowing
in a moonlit floral dance.
An old man ordering a bride?

Till rising up from Feb's cold ground
Felt reluctance of her legs to stand.
Would she sustain the waiting game
Thin white roots to snake the soil
Leaves look out from that brown grave.
Watch the buds bulge on each stem.
Open, hungry for the sun.

But she didn't wait alone,
flying in, the lily beetle,
an alien orange lily eater.
The lily beetle, so particular,
allergic to all other plants,
how did it track her lilies down?
How does an anteater find ants?

Flew in on wings bright as the petals,
cancelling the flower show.
At least they made a meal of it,
and their timing was precise.

HORTS

The red stems of the convolvulous
spread across the paving, of gravestones, like writing.
The original memorials already eroded.
What is it trying to say, this weedy graffiti,
that life goes on, even on stony ground.
Not if, but what, moves into this niche market.

The bee enters the white trumpet flower,
as behind me in Horts
old men play big instruments
filling the bar with jazz.
Traditional tunes I've heard before
musicians I've known for four decades or more
tunes that bypassed my fragile music centre
have entered the hard drive of my brain.
Have got to know the bar staff,
say Hello to regulars, bagged our table.
We play cards enclosed in wood panelling
where once judges discussed decisions,
decided lives, a wig and pen preserved
in a frame on the wall, where aphorisms e.g.
"Hope is a good breakfast but a bad supper."
lose out to the big screen
showing match of the day.

Across the road the law courts
are Sunday silent.
The clock on the old city gateway
goes on recording the hours
adding up its long sums.
The first Queen Elizabeth the came this way
admired our tall church,
St. Mary Redcliffe, despite the tower,
being unfinished in her day.

Did citizens now buried
in bindweed scribbled graves
consult its hands on errands that seemed
important then, as now, the band
discuss this lunchtime's session,
packing amplifiers and guitar cases
into the boots of cars.

CROSSED LINES

Nearly forty years since that pretty baby
erupted into our lives, disrupted our lives.
As we left our teens behind, the century in its sixties
Swinging, they said, we were too near the apex.
Could any other baby have behaved like this?
No, the human race would never have got past first base.
Every rule of those unruly first years broken.
We held his hand, or letting go,
we lost him, and we missed him.

'Well he was here a minute ago.
Yes, literally, I don't know, he could be anywhere,
Jane said she saw him on the road to Portishead.'
There are no pavements on the road to Portishead.
We feared for him who had no fear
or his fears misplaced saw no danger from
car's thrust, water's depth, or intent of stranger.

Would he ever come out of the Gents
dare I go in and rescue him, my blue eyed boy?
Had someone been tempted by trusting hand,
clear skin, request for assistance
or was he just wrecking the plumbing?

We had no name for his differences
only knew we were sidelined, cut off, walked alone.
Country lane, cliff path, snowy field, crowded beach
shopping mall, 'Charlie will find us.'
'Charlie doesn't know where we are.'
'Lets go home,' If I was going home
I wouldn't have started from here.
Life was full of Irish directions
signposts all askew.
Time didn't teach us new tricks
but honed up on the ones we knew.

Walking the years till the years put a brake on
us all, roads less promising, hills steeper,
gates locked, cliff path out of reach.
But it brought us a lifeline too.
Now as an October afternoon stretches
too soon into evening, leaves turn into litter,
and radio is full of war.
I pick up my mobile to say
'We're here.' 'Where's here?'
'Well we turned left by the King William
but that was ages ago. I think we're
near the airport, the planes are flying low.'
'Give me some landmarks, what can you see?'
'There's an awfully nice beech hedge,'
'I mean like the name of the road,'
'God knows, something rural, Oak Hill, Frog Lane.'
'Stay where you are, I'll get the car.'
What I like about mobiles is
no one need ever get lost again?

TIME AND TIDE

From this window where,
fishermen waited for tides to rise,
wives waited for men to return
fish-rich from local seas.
I can see the sheep heaped under the hedge on the hill,
watch them disperse like baby spiders
from a disturbed web. The young ones,
moving surprisingly fast,
running towards their chosen grass
like carnivores, as though,
expecting it to run away.

The blue tits, nesting again
in the hole in the wall, the male,
pausing on a narrow plank protruding
from the fence, an aerial kerb, is anything coming?
Waiting with something small and green in his beak.
It won't go far among a blue tit brood.
But the parent birds make many trips
to the bounty of high morning banks.
while I watch the tidal river make
a silver road through green pastures,
where brown cows graze the flat field by the bridge
as if looking at an old picture on a pub wall

The pictures on the pub wall are all of ships.
The Armada came this way.
A ship went down; it's wreckage used to beam
the Village Inn. So many since have come to grief.
Yesterday we were marooned for nine hours
in an open boat waiting for high tide
to lift us off our mud island.

The leggy birds came, oyster catchers,
a little egret paddled past. a heron fished.
Speckled birds that hurried,
as if they too feared sinking, weren't designed
to find, rich pickings, in the mud
that captured us. Turned our motor off.
Prisoners, while all around experienced sailors
raced by in deeper channels,
going home to moored yachts.

It was dark when the tide finally arrived,
our oars splashed in moonlit waves
as though we had braved big seas
to sneak a smuggled cargo in
or find asylum from an aggressive regime.
Risked our lives between
the soft mud and the dark water?

WORM'S TURN

On top of the snow a rigid worm,
the colour of meat, shaped
like a butchers hook.
New evidence exposed by this white field.
Where, otherwise, only the foot and paw prints
of one man and his dog disturb new world.

Hazel, Beech and Oak, already
dripping in the woods. Last night
this sudden snowstorm brought
excitement to the streets.
One white hour, twelth night.

On the City Centre they'd been
taking down the lights.
Only fat snowmen remained,
suspended above the lamp posts.
Their plastic scarves overlaid
with the cold truth. People
leaving early, making tracks.
I stayed on till closing time
watched the side roads turn to slush.

This morning I'm surprised
that so much snow has stayed
altering the local landscape,
setting up worm's little tragedy.

Flattened in parts, perhaps it was
dropped from a beak to lie
so awkwardly, so obvious. Provide,
another bright eyed bird with lunch.

My feet, already wet, I scrape a hole.
Reveal grass underneath. Then with
same foot, manoeuvre bent remains.
Watch worm slide into green grave.

This should be, end of story.
But find I'm at a resurrection.
The worm turns, stretches
earth to earth. I go on my way rejoicing
despite reflecting, that for a worm
life is mainly burying yourself.

DONKEY WORK

When I was young donkeys were more relevant.
Probably because we all read the bible
Where donkeys often got a mention,
Not only when taking
Mary & Joseph to the stable
An appropriate destination for a donkey
even when there isn't a famous baby involved.
Probably its finest hour.

Mostly they were more like a train
Taking not only people but their luggage
over rough terrain, certainly a donkey
was indispensable in so many lands.
And so often confined to stony ground.

The donkeys in Weston on the other hand
Were there for our enjoyment, as we arrived
by bus, car or Sunday school outing charabanc
and sat down with our sandwiches beside the pier
to spend our pocket money on a ride.
I was always afraid the donkey man
would make them run. Something other
children enjoyed but I preferred mine
to be called Dobbin not Flash.

It wasn't the mountain pass or Bethlehem
this little stretch of sand but scary enough
for me, buying a moment of obduracy,
to share the donkeys trek through history.
By then I'd found there was a discrepancy between
What happened in books and what happened on holiday
a gulf even a donkey couldn't cross.

But at least they were real animals
who pushed against their harnesses, bared
enormous teeth, needed to eat
as well as make hay while the sun shone.
for the donkey men, on the beach.
When it was time for us to go home
the donkeys too were loaded into lorries
taken to green fields, their solid shapes
merging in with cows and sheep.
They'd done their job.
They'd earned their keep.

MISSING

At first I thought each day
would fatten the wedge between
your death, my life, soften
that hard line cutting time in two.
Open the door wider,
let new light cut through the shade
rain and wind rush in, this stain,
washed a thousand times,
left out in sun and rain,
grow pale, blend in.

Its not like that, more as though
a pretty experiment
the dye run through, would always show
how it must work, again and again.
Whoever discovered, the circulation
of the blood say, knew it must stand true,
be taken into account
with more sophisticated surgery.

This memory of you
I half know, half invent
will run my lifetime through.
Blossom on this hawthorn tree
one year thick as clotted cream
the bee's confused, the next,
less generous, letting in the sky.
Still hardy enough to withstand,
weather's buffeting, brambles invasion,
the old wall caving in.

The seasons have performed their usual tricks.
The ability of trees
to change their mood, their dress
adapt to nakedness.
Survive so many absences.

The world has changed its attitudes
and I've moved my allegiances.
But your absence from your life
and mine, touches everything.
No harvest since make good.
No other pain out sting.

NO WAY

House arrest. Windowed in
prisoners denied the spring.
Hardly dare to peer over hedges.
We are the unclean, plague carriers,
a belled leper more self confidence.

The fields subdued, sheep ruled.
cordoned off by sick animals.
Medieval, our lives decided
by an infected pig, contiguous cow
and healthy deer lest they defect.
Unhappy breed of ungulates

No one can go to the country.
and the country can't go to town.
We borrow badger habits, burrow down.

Fenced off by farming, the smoke
of burning carcasses doesn't miss a screen,
a dirty war, the map spread out
to follow disease spreading flags.
Where was the murderer last seen?

It comes in on our tyre tracks, it comes in
on the wind. Clean booted the golfers'
follow their ball from green to green,
worker, trucker and tourist all suspects.

We cull it back like grass, but it
overtakes our murder squads, outwits
our funeral pyres. We who've beaten
and bred fellow mammals
into meat and obedience, fingers burnt.
Still can't withdraw. Hardwired as the flock
following the bellweather
into the valley of death.

THE HORSELESS RIDER

Slowing down behind a girl on a horse
her jodpurred mate walking beside her,
Charlie, driver complains
of horses on the road.
How unsuited to traffic,
how dangerous it is for driver and rider.
I say, 'Horses were here before cars
and you're not paid to police the planet,
or people intended to live forever.'
Guy, autistic son says, 'I can't see
the other horse though?'
'That's because there isn't one,'
I state the bleeding obvious.
'They're sharing,' Charlie, father says, as I
attempt to illustrate the point
with Aesops's fable
of father and son leading a horse
till the people say.
'Two men walking when they have a horse?'
The father rides.
'That man riding while his poor boy walks.'
The son rides. People criticise,
'Young man riding while an old man walks.'
They both ride. 'Poor horse.'
They carry the horse.
'Stupid men,' the people cry.
I say, 'The moral is you can't please everyone,
don't even try.'
Guy says, 'A horse is heavier than you think.'

You can take them to water
but you can't make them drink.

BURGH ISLAND

Here where two tides divide,
both going out to leave
sand dunes in the damp May dusk.
Each white lipped wave rushing forward
to say goodbye
to the one across the bay
each surge forward takes
it further away.

Young birds in steep flower coated lanes
Flutter to the other bank
Make it against a multiple of odds.

We who reached the Pub
feet sinking in wet sand,
slipping on green slimed rocks,
watery inlets still swirling round our feet,
not sure which way to go. Watch
Landrovers with local timing
drive over, knowing the camber
of dry sand is ready for their weight.

Coming through the rain
in the approaching dark.
White as ambulances
as if to the rescue of
some storm tossed ship.

Urgency evaporates in the Pilchard where
we sit beside a stuffed green parrot
who died in 1979 but looks like
its been dead longer than that.
Lived in lustier centuries
remembers cruel hook handed cap'ns
blue coated shoulder
scarred with it's talons.

From the round window
I can see how much easier
it will be to get back.

DEATH OF A PRINCESS

Look your last on all things lovely
Walter de la Mere advised.
Ah but he didn't realize
How we would live by images
a thousand pictures replace.
The thousand words
run over page after page after page
Transfer to screen, download
so there is no ending.

Our icons remain
As we first knew them
Smiling from our screens.
Twenty years since Elvis died
All the other weekend
His sexuality still splayed
above and below his guitar
like some eternal orgasm.

Now the death of Diana
Shocks us awake, disturbs
our Sunday morning.
Diana dead, it cant be true?
Just another press release,
the shattered car in the underpass, perhaps
but not her body on a plane?

Why look at her now.
Smiling so sympathetically
at the man with Aids
Cradling the girl with a black bulb
where a useful limb should be.
Could the princess who had long legs
that did so much for expensive dresses understand?
She seemed to. Crumpled bride and skiing mother
Looking up with Bambi eyes
at the latest interview.

'Such a sad life I wouldn't
have wanted it,' says the woman buying
a paper in my local Newsagents.
'Wouldn't you? What were you doing
on Saturday night?
Odds on not dining at the Paris Ritz
with your playboy lover.'
Ok not everyone's cup of tea
And the price turned out to be
Higher than expected but..
nice work if you can qualify.

And still they come
deep and deeper, the flowers lie
turning London's green
into something in between
a garden and a compost heap
half sweet, half polythene
ill wind that blows,
more softly on the florists.
And still they weep
Who thought they knew her,
sure she cared, held every hand
had there been world enough and time?

LYNMOUTH

Coming down the cliff path
We can only see, waves perm beach,
old cottages festooned with drought bright geraniums,
thatched Pub. It still looks like
the pictures in Lynton museum about the flood

Noah didn't live here, but one day
this river lost it's temper,
dragged people and houses down
in well recorded tantrum to the sea.
Made headlines in my parochial childhood.
oh the human interest
of an almost local Act of God.

Today it passes harbour boat,
greets with equanimity, evening tide.
Once ptaradactyls rose, where
gulls perfectly evolved catch crusts,
stylish scavengers who've come
so far for crumbs.

Close up watch weed flecked wave turn,
spray stones. Bits of glass bashed opaque.
One dead gull lies decomposing
in sea's swell, beak open,
skin apparent, resembling early birds
breaking the flight path in.

All other litter is ours.
Plastic squeeze shapes trace tideline.
Dismembered doll plays at tragedy.
A group of boys make for the harbour wall.
up, over, no hurdle this.
Our son will he attempt...
already anticipating failure
Legs strong and straight as theirs
won't lever him over.

The too loud, too ready call
for our assistance, aftermath
as strangers turn to look, then look away.
Modify my reactions in advance,
make allowances, for them, for him, for me.
But he dismisses impossible obstacle
Backtracks to common entrance

This glass once sharp, new broken, clear
how many tides did it take
for pebbles and water to blur, reshape?
Was that dead gull one who couldn't catch?
Time and tide meet their match.
flaws contained, tools to cancel out
our weaknesses. He joins boys
throwing stones to skim sea's surface
hit dancing drink can. Drags the fattest
pebble from it's muddy bed
to drop short of target,
only just misses boys.
At least he makes a splash.

On the cliff path lean against sea view
From here discrepancy not show
Though down on the beach could see
Every drastic ripple flow
From that first disastrous throw

WHILE THERE'S MUSIC

Its hot it in the Old Duke
The singer belts out the blues
a woman with attitude,
plus voice, coming across,
at home with an audience
confident even without the applause
all hands clapping, calling for more

My red wine doesn't taste right.
'Same again.' 'No I'll have a white.'
But reluctant to waste the remains
of the Merlot I pour it into
the fresh glass of Chardonnay.
Where it disperses slowly
But perfectly as though rehearsed
coloring the new wine completely
like a medical diagnosis.
Blood in the urine
telling sick jokes?

The bar staff are collecting the glasses
the band packing instruments into
cases, each case designed particularly,
it all fits. Two old men high on
beer, music and conversation
order a taxi on mobile phones
then reach behind their chairs for walking sticks
shuffle out carefully negotiating familiar hazards.

The singer looks more ordinary
without her song, pulling her coat on
covering the sparkly frock

SWINGS AND ROUDABOUTS

In the arcade the children play the slots.
The little ones crowd round an old favourite
where a crane swings out,
lowers, opens up to grab
a soft toy trapped in a transparent cage.

Preset to fail, merely grazes
the rainbow teddy, blue giraffe.
The coin drops. The crane
folds up and puts itself away.
Until…. played again and again
its metal claws, encircle, grasp,
a yellow elephant against the odds
or, contrived law of averages?
Opens up, to drop, outside the box.
The child collects;

Going back along the narrow road
from Port Gaverne, driving between high banks
of moon daisies, stitchwort, buttercups.
May's flora glowing in late evening light.
Into our wind screen a white owl,
rises up on hinged wings,
holds up a mouse, its little death
displayed, against the backdrop of full moon.

We are suitably impressed.
Fat wings flap smoothly, take the owl
Back into the thickening dark,
disappearing gently like an unalarming ghost.
Somewhere in barn or Oak
chicks will test new beaks' efficiency
the rodent's little tragedy, securing,
survival for another night.

We too are making tracks,
prepared, packages of fish and chips
Warming my lap, meanwhile we share
our headlights with the moths.

POND LIFE

Waterlily leaves don't fade
but brighten to gold,
like the ruddy carp moving together
as though they'd rehearsed all year.
Simple shapes turning slowly
but particularly in the dark water
To a tune I cannot hear

They say fish are therapeutic
restore your soul like trees
certainly these look relaxing
ghosting down, down,
disappearing gently,
like dead relatives.

Big fish eat the little fish
tidy as Russian dolls.
This one isn't satisfied
comes up to bite the air
ambitious beyond its habitat
independent of the shoal.
A big fish in a little pond
where does it go from here?

Maybe its not so peaceful
what goes on down there
down below the surface
among the roots and snails.
But here in Hillside Nursery
distracted by plants for sale,
we don't look beyond the surface
the rain is all we share.

PROVIDENCE LANE

My Neck of the Woods

From war baby to pensioner I've lived,
on this same hill, the Somerset side
of Brunel's Suspension bridge.

This was 'our hill,' where we laid down
our skipping rope, one end tied to the lamppost
the other held by one of us.
Me, Pat, Olwen or Hilary spanning
the road, laid down to let
an occasional car go by.

Parking is our problem now
Cars squeeze past each other on the brow.

This was 'our field', its terrain made interesting
by a legacy of underground passages
old miners left behind. Canyons
we called these red mud ditches
Climbed into their tunnelled depths
Below the roots of trees, when
iron ore was king, mined by men,
still pictured on pub wall
who died and left their caves behind,
along with the odd artefact, a lamp, shovel, pick
the rest, was blackberries and primroses.
Now tall evergreens, planted in my teens
cast a flowerless shade and only pigeons nest
though beyond them bluebells mark the ridge
between, pine trees dark canopy
and beeches making new leaves from old wood.

A buzzard hangs above the little wilderness
Across the road where half a century's
neglect hid ruined cottages. Gorse,
brambles, blackthorn, an apple tree
housed, bullfinch, robin, thrush
where Mr Wilmot laid foundations
for a house never made.
Mr Wilmot's died at last
tamed now his little wilderness
to make way for a new housing estates.
JCB's lift scoops full of wormy earth
a blackbird's beak could only dream on.
Eat up the banks where lizards
sunbathed in my schooldays.

Today I saw a deer picking its delicate way
among the concrete foundations of a new house.
Deer were only a promise when big boys said
How they were up there, in the woods
Older siblings lifted me up to peer through holes
a recent war had fashioned in the wall,
for soldiers to shoot through, the big boys said.
Private then, trespassers would be prosecuted.
Now dog walkers and manmade cycle tracks
big balloons and global kites
hover over common ground
where larks still nest

I never saw deer then, foxes were commoner
our enemies, when every garden had a hen run.
Now I've heard deer are becoming a pest
Whereas as I feel dislocated, lost in my own backyard.
Though at home in the Miners Rest.

RECESSION 2008-FL.

How cold it is, even with the sun
shafting the frosty lawn,
solid bird bath doesn't respond to robin thirst.
How soon the early dark
cuts short the afternoon.
Night forever on its back.

How quickly the tinsel
and wrapping paper are tidied away.
The black sack conceals but cant destroy
the evidence of our recent indulgences.
Landfill overflows and waste
has lost its market place.

Otherwise we have been warned
2009 comes in on a bad vibe.
The banks are shrinking
The shops are shutting
The Pubs are closing
Sterling has lost it clout
The good times shrouded
in more than this cold mist
that tricks the view away.

Every news report we get
And they are many, full of forebodings
Dotted with war and pestilence
The smoke from too many fires
never quite put out.

Old grievances that justify new weaponry.
Nothing goes and history makes its own detritus
lying in the road, blocking our way.

Death by intent or accident
Last year's parade of the famously departed.
2008, their closing date.

The lucky ones who made three score years and ten
whose names we knew, their talents displayed again.
The parts they played, the goals they scored,
the lives they saved, portraits, taken when young
passed round the media again.

But we are in recession.
In recession from what?
The fat times, we sat out,
didn't anticipate the lean years?
Had forgotten the biblical stories.
The bubbles that burst when touched.
Emperors clothes that cant be worn again
A fashion we only imagined
So what were we eating
and wearing and sleeping in,
upgrading our kitchens and changing
our tunes, building conservatories to catch the sun
that was only a trick of the light.

They are going, going…the illusions of prosperity.
Where are the comedians, the magicians,
the medical miracles offering
to ease us out of this bad seat,
we once felt so lucky to secure
as we watched the old year out.
Limp in to greet this new calendar,
already reminding us,
of appointments with bad tidings.

SEEING RED ON THE M4

The banks are overgrown, the trees in full leaf
merge, in green uniform of high summer.
Only cut grass turns fields harvest gold,
like the shorn sheep, innocence lost,
making small inroads into lush grasses.
The cows chew down to yellow roots.
Here a field of flax making blue horizons
close enough to touch.
And there red poppies spatter
blood stain the edges of ripening wheat
An occasional haemorrhage
drenching the maincrop.

Long days of June, time rich we relax.
The poppies have crossed the dual carriageway,
strayed into the central reservation
where a rabbit seeking new pastures
changes its mind, leaps suddenly
to retrack, make it back to full fields.

Charlie brakes, miscalculates its speed
as it bounds beneath our wheels.
I feel the bump of its demise.
The body flung back
into oncoming traffic.

Our car goes on to Oxford
passing other roadkill, a hawk's
messed feathers, a young fox.
But we aren't shocked,
by these other carcasses,
They're not ours. Part of the bigger picture.
We're all running against the odds.
The car radio recording news of young men
caught in the crossfire of human conflict,
their mourning families,
nothing will ever put right.

But still the rabbit, the death bump.
My mind, takes a copy, files
with bigger tragedies, less recent,
though securely locked, time can't decode
but for now, replaced, by that last leap.

SEATS

These seats like useful gravestones
are set conveniently about our beauty spots.
overlooking the sea, the beach, the cliff, the lake.
Weary walkers or impromptu picnickers
can take a break, read the inscription.
How Henry sat here, and so loved the view.
That now he wants to share with you.
Henry who died in 1999, aged 62
And never saw the millennium fireworks
Breaking up us his patch of sky
That today is blue.

Betty and Alan remembered by their children
who walked this way before us.
Louise born after me, dead already
How she loved it here, that last holiday
I think of Anne Bronte photographed
against the Scarborough cliffs.

Then there's James, younger than our son
Taken tragically from this tranquil place.
Did he fall or jump from these impressive cliffs?
Where now we eat our sandwiches.

Along the river Dart, in Kingsbridge
So many seats, so many citizens who sat
and watched boat laden tide rise and subside,
fed the ducks and inadvertently
the ancestors of these greedy gulls
perched on each beached boat
taking their pick of everything.

Perhaps the saddest stories are untitled.
Nameless seats where only an indent
in the wood remains to show
someone who was loved and mourned enough
to be considered worthy of a seat.
But who was here where now we watch
the sun go down making a silver road
from horizon to shore for
the red sailed yachts to cross.
Just these four small holes
where the nails went in.

SLAD

Slad smells of garlic,
though looks more kempt
than Laurie Lee described it.
A long time since I read the book
but surely something more abandoned
than this disciplined display.

We find his grave, not very old
light coloured, embroidered with stone flowers.
A poem on the back and bright primroses,
we used to call polyanthus, cover the mound.
Yellow natives, softer but more prolific
still hold the bank above.

A conversation overheard in the Pub.
'I got some in £ Stretchers.'
'How much?'
'Two ninety nine.'
Sounds out of tune, like the magenta primroses
no longer prim nor rose.

The gardens are all lawn daisied and spring flowered.
A fat bee is spoilt for choice.
Geese won't pose, come up to hiss my camera
like a harassed princess, or a celebrity leaving rehab.
A green woodpecker flies across the landscape
disappears into a shapely Oak.

By the pond, a walkway, planted with daffodils.
There's lots of daffodils, the houses are all well kept.
A tabby cat joins me on the oblong stone
belonging to James Irewood, who lived and died,
before, Laurie Lee arrived to taste the cider.

Beyond minding about me and the cat
sitting on his embossed cross.
The elaborate writing running round,
the skeleton beneath, as the sun
goes behind a cloud, closes up the celandines,
and we drive into Stroud.

THE STARLINGS OF MEARE

We left the Duke about three in the afternoon.
The sun came with us, shone in our eyes
obscuring the view of yellow hedges.
Driving through the last of October
in search of ornithology.
Rooks flapping like falling leaves,
the raggedness of it.

After passing Glastonbury's manmade hill
Sticking up among flat fields of Somerset
the level landscape heaped with sheep
We found the signpost to Meare at last.

A cloud of starlings crossed our path.
We drew up in a layby.
It was what we'd come for.
Watched the starlings pulse the sky
like an echocardiogram, before,
sagging the telegraph wires
and painting a barn roof black.

In Meare we parked in the car park
We weren't alone in the approaching dark.
Followed the wellington boots of others
along the sanctuary path
straight down the line, it was a railway once
with railway things still lying around
A station here where milk churns were loaded
by men in uniforms. And men in hats
made a last dash for the train to town
and people carried oblong cases and bags

Today they all have binoculars, or dogs, or children,
or all three. I wish I'd brought binoculars to see
the starlings, they're flying so low,
disappearing into the reed beds
more like a swarm of insects than birds.
Its easy to believe in evolution
Here in the Somerset dusk

'Will they fly up again? I ask
the woman with the binoculars.
Zooming in with my camera,
They could still be anything
black dotting the horizon like a puzzle game.
'Not till dawn,' she says,
'its the biggest starling roost
in the country, in England probably.'
'The world,' I suggest.
Not quite impressed enough.

In the Railway Inn we're met
by a lifesize wax undertaker
who talks to us, and turns his head.
There's a convincing ghost
by the television who screams and rattles his chains
if you clap your hands.
Guy, our son, claps his frequently.
The locals have lost interest.
A green faced witch on a broom
performs similar tricks by the fruit machine.
When we go to the bar, Dracula starts up.
Cobwebs hang from the window and faces peer in.
Its Halloween and the Railway Inn
is thoroughly bewitched.

Its dark outside and the starlings
have all settled down for the night.
The man behind us leans over to take a photo
Not of the shuddering ghost or black art flocks.
But the television screen showing,
football results, next week's fixtures.

WINDOWS

Woken from disturbed dreams
where the dead walk again
but have lost their place, their time, their relevance
fit uneasily into the unfamiliar bed,
in the new room tacked onto the old cottage.
How well placed the four windows framed in pale wood.
Thick weave cotton curtains, barely blue,
draw back on each different view.

The cottage opposite, the wide river,
can almost figure out tide times?
The hill where I used to watch the sheep
being herded by dogs, now almost obscured
by the fig tree with its big foreign leaves.
On the other side the reconstructed garden
patio and rockery, bamboo gone native
but the old apple tree still in situ,
where the blackbird sang in spring.

No blossom today, we came late this year. Hard
green apples or brown ones rotten on the bough.
The tiny stone building with church windows,
saved, as though, someone still prayed
stored more than old garden implements,
discarded plastic chairs.

I can't remember where I too belong.
Go to the garden window to see,
if the dawn comes in this way?
It is still black night and don't expect
to see this light. Bright but sinister somehow
as though a silver man, the paint not dry
had smeared himself across the sky.
Whatever separates heaven and earth
torn aside, spoiling the eventual surprise?

But these stars are a surprise, coming on them suddenly
their unearthly brightness. Like young love
lifting you onto another planet
you could hardly believe
that such a thing happened
though everyone had promised
and it was common knowledge.
But you weren't amazed it didn't last.

NEWS ITEM

Someone has stolen a Stegosuarus's footprints
probably the only ones.
Why?
Because they were there,
Because they could, we have the technology
to drill through rock undisturbed
for a hundred and forty million years
and we have the footprints to prove it
letting us know Steg was here.
surer than "Daisy 4 Jack" sprayed
on the lavatory wall.

Probably an ordinary Jurassic sort of morning
when Steg made his way
one foot in front of the other
not knowing they were here to stay.
Well, till today.

Who would want a Stegosauruses footprint
carved out of Australian rock,
letting us know it was part of the landmass?
that 'saurus's strode where oceans wave now.

What do you do with the footprints?
Easier to store in the basement than the attic.
"What have you got in that sports bag?
Looks heavy."
"The footprints of a Stegosaurus."
"Of course silly me, buy one get one free."

Even if they put them back
it won't be the same.
Even if the Stegosaurus knew
stepping aside to avoid a puddle
(beginnings of the Pacific perhaps)
or acknowledge a Brontosaurus
browsing on an unnamed plant.
"Cold morning, backbone playing up.
Ice age on the way?"
"Ice age? Its not even snowing."
Going off in a huff,
stamping his feet in the mud
"that'll show em."

IN A NUTSHELL

Sparrows fall
and decompose
But nothing ever really goes.

SUSPENSION BRIDGE

'Whass think of 'ee then?
A grand sight innit.'
'Yeah, a 'eritige site even.'
'Put Bristol on the map.'
'Bristols always bin on the map,
well since they've 'ad maps.'

'Since when did they 'ave maps?'
'Bet they 'ad maps in ancient Greece,
Chinal even.' 'Bet Bristol weren't on that.
Bet it were just the Great Wall.'
'And Bible lands, 'ad to get across the desert.'

'Ardly need an Atlas, just yonder star.'
'Don't ask I?
Didn't say it were the bleedin pyrimids.
But Isambard did that.'

'Isambard did everything round 'ere.'
'Everythign?'
'Well ev'rything whats to do with transport
The iron boat, Temple Meads, the railway track.'
'an a bridge for the cars to go over the Avon.'

'Not cars, there weren't none,
not when he built it, 1864.'
'Says 'ere 'ee died in 1859
someone else must 'ave built it.'

'Well he 'ad the ideer.'
'But 'ee didn't even see it,
'ee wouldn't even know it was still 'ere.
'ee wouldn't even know it was ever 'ere.'

'Get a surprise if 'ee came back.
all them boats going under it
and all them cars goin over it.'
'Yeah, 'specially the cars.'

THE NEEDLE TREE

That beech I called the needle tree
Where two branches crossed paths permanently.
Welded together, then parted.
Went their separate ways
Then met again, conjoined to make an eye.
A dress makers daughter, I,
Would to fill that gap
with more than sky.

Now the victim of
a chainsaw massacre
in these managed woods.
The damaged and misshapen,
Sacrificed to the greater good?
Here where the deer venture cautiously.
Not off limits but outside their comfort zone
But horse riders have signposts of their own
and men extend the cycle way.

Seasons cover up the spaces.
New year, new growth.
Maybe its only I who remember
how that particular tree overcame
its disability. Grew to maturity.

Nature allows for differences.
Evolution thrives on possibilities.
Machinery on the other hand
moves in fits and starts
goes too fast to test
how one thing may affect the rest.

The ones who missed the sign posts,
left bereft of options, going nowhere
as if life wasn't also, waiting at bus stops

Do whatever gods there be, wish
they'd given us less options?
Or we'd shown less initiative
just let things be. No we were born
to interfere, make room for our fecundity
thread the eye of a needle tree.

OUTLIVED

"Wait for me?" You'd stopped
to use the phone box at the bottom of the hill.
I looked back to wait for you
stood on the bend of the road
where I live now, fifty years on.

The blondes, brunettes and redheads
coded by the colour of their hair.
Yours platinum like Marilyn
striking against the astrakhan collar
of the black coat, buttonless,
pulled round, hugging your curves.
Hiding your curves, but provocative
Drawing attention.
It didn't look as though,
made by our mother, nor did you.
Looking too sophisticated
for this village hill. More the girl made good,
looking up her roots?
Finding they no longer matched.

CLOTHES LIVE AFTER US

Perhaps I'm self obsessed
As when the woman at work died
I remembered the compliment.
How once she'd admired my new dress.
Or was it the cashmere cardigan,
I thought I'd paid too much for, justified.
Made my day.
The flesh is weak
and though the music stops
red shoes
dance on.

ST. MARY REDCLIFFE

Thomas Chatterton was born here,
in this square house
opposite St. Mary Redcliffe,
monument to stone's possibilities.
A short life but intense.
Born under the wing of history and architecture,
effigies of dead saints his playmates.

What leap of faith kick started this hard edifice?
This monument to man's sheer doggedness?
Who first aspired to invest so much of their belief
to set an airy afterlife in stone
make it flow like an expensive dress.
Roped in surveyors, draughtsmen, masons
Stayed with it till the tower rose above
The burghers houses, river industry
to make us feel inadequate
like looking up at the night sky
reduced by stars and galaxies
unsure of where we stand
in this vast pecking order.

Yet men built this church,
To the glory of God,
A god we're not quite so sure of
as those old Bristolians, yet here it stands
defying shifting faiths and time's long stride.
Avoiding recent wars stone shattering bombs
Admired by that icon of British History
Queen Elizabeth the first.
'The fairest, goodliest and most famous ...'
Did that bright boy, Tom Chatterton,
die deliberately? Had he expected more
of life and London after growing up immersed
in this, amazing church.

THE GOLF SEAT

Up here without my i phone
reliant on local props.
This wooden bench, the very one.
Where we used to play, built in perspective
Graded like a swimming pool
We walked the plank.
From low start to raised end.
Then jump. Here where
the wild scabious grew and purple stuff
beloved by butterflies. Still do.

Came here with Hilary and Hetty
in those long school holidays
Both dead, my sister long ago.
Yet still too soon to talk about.
Auntie Hetty in old age, when
the Lockerbie bombing was making news.
Who once defied a golfer telling us off
for making too much noise.
She came from town and didn't know
golfers were king round here

Today glad to just sit, see how late September
tans beeches. A poem abut death that impressed me
when young, said, "Who wants to be
the last leaf on the tree?' Oh no, not me
I would go in common gust.
One swirling stormy night, all blow.

Not so sure now, want to stay and watch
the dew laid out to dry across the greens.
Seeping quietly into my Reeboks.
Auntie Hetty took her shoes off
when we were picking blackberries.
Bramble's black fruit still gleams
Through curtains of spider webs
But I've no urge to gather
or a mother to accept, needing to stain
the apples pink in our Sunday tart.

WINTER REDS

The poinsettia is a little the worse for wear
but its colour persists.
Oblivious of new calendars,
Christmas is Christmas past,
the decorations taken down.
Flaunting still its original colouring
paradigm red, against the dark leaf,
following the contours of the leaf
where leaf and petal meet
A scarlet leaf in flowery disguise
Could have fooled me.

So many in the supermarkets
Making them look cheap
They are cheap, easy to germinate
as in their native land
blood stain a whole hillside.
But here in my living room
in dull January, exotic, tropical.

Outside driving through the winter countryside
All gardens look untended, deserted almost
In the fields wool coloured sheep,
Move slowly heavy with lambs.
Muddy walks not yet interrupted
by the joy of violet's shy arrival
or any sign of primroses.
Only a red phone box
Also looking the worse for wear
Its colour too persists
though no one comes anymore
to call, lover or doctor
explain their absence to friends or relatives
Arrange another meeting?

So much went on in phone boxes
Now the whole world in our hands
Friends and relatives a finger tip away.

The whole landscape looks defunct until
A fox slinks across the road, slips
into the bank, creating a little drama
of warm fur and bad intentions.

On the car's audio tape
Alan Bennet's diaries recall,
a fox finding spectacular cover in Hyde Park
among Princess Diana's memorial flowers,
teddy bears and polythene.
How far away it seems
that makeshift graveyard scene
that frantic mourning.

VERANDA

So many birds come to our veranda
we hardly need the wooden toucan
though Duncan hangs his swim wear on its beak.
The birds are foreign to us
but we give them English names
like everything else in Barbados.

Yellow robins and titian pigeons.
sparrows and finches our instant friends
hop across the white boards, brave our table.
The greediest are starling sized black birds
Their shrill cries wake us, gimme, gimme,
more cheese, more cheese.

Offer no song in exchange, sharp shapes displaying
upturned tails in a ritual dance;
Flying up from the spiky tropical branches
that catch the water from the sudden storms.
One long beaked loner sits aloof, hunched
on a separate tree, with leaves
cut like paper lanterns, painted green.

From the balcony we survey our private jungle
Monkeys swinging from the big bean trees
run up the fences to negotiate
barbed wire with monkey expertise.

How quickly the towels dry
when we come back from the beach
sit drinking G and T's, glasses rimmed with lime
as Duncan tries to keep the standards up.
Notice the big hawk moth chasing the fan
till it alights exhausted on the wooden ceiling
A Gecko matching the pale ceiling, as gecko's do
still as the wooden toucan
so we think it too is a decoration, argue,
till, it picks up neat feet
moves with sudden animation
blows its camouflage
to show an interest in the big moth.

Big moth unaware of its predator, the tiny dinosaur,
lively fossil closing in, brushes the winged body
then moves away, no longer hungry
or just disappointed. This promising meal
not to his taste after all.
The moth alerted, flits again,
pretends to be chasing the light
not running away.

The tree frogs have already started.
They'll sing all night as we nurse rum and cokes
that cost less than the imported crisps
try to rearrange the world more to our liking,
as though we didn't sit, close to paradise,
lit with stars and fireflies,
but more than the mosquito's bite
gets under our skin.

NORTH CORNWALL, 2010

The bounty of the banks
is shadowed on the road
gold weeds, red campion and vetch
making summer patterns, black on grey.

Moon, the tide maker, heaps water into waves
ploughs serrated sea as each wave tries
to make it to the beach or breaks
early, to be seized on by surfers, bagging a ride.
Eager as my camera to pick the right moment.
Its an age difference.
So many things are.

We struggle over rocks
where once we played.
It is so hot today, a tropical beach
complete with lone umbrella hiding a body?
An Agatha Christie novel as Cornwall's sea,
draws a curved edge basks in Caribbean weather.
Air fares not included.

Till driving to another cove, may's flowers,
balancing above blue sea
Deep valleys still sport Bluebells and late primroses.
Birds foot trefoil clings to rock.
In cottage gardens daisied lawns all black birded.

Not all is prettiness, green trees disfigured by
old winters, bend away from walls.
Sails of generators set to farm the wind
grind slowly as the law, the wind is out of season.
Brown cows browse and tractors block
the lanes, they're sat outside at Port William
everyone's taking photos; Sunset over Atlantic.
This is the end of England, its warmest spot.
Ripens our skins like fruit
and Guy's lost watch has left,
a white bracelet round his wrist.

WAVES OF TREBARWITH

Fierce and unfriendly the white waves
surge up this little creek
but tied to moon's authority fail to reach
our viewing rock, despite looking
desperate enough to leapfrog this beach.
Ignore old laws, safe spots,
pick us up and toss into the boiling pot
like the last act of some betrayed old Greek.

The rocks are legless, can't run for cover
hit perpetually, each wave momentarily obliterates
saturates in their foamy wake
that drains back in a patterning
determined by the rocks relief.
Scars, proof of previous tide's torture
but who can afford to take the Atlantic to court?

So many times this excited water
splashed to cliff top as it attempts to reduce
the slatey walls, taming their obduracy.
Though sun and season hardened
might still break down tonight.
This tide's taking a crack at it,
easing in like a rat.

Notices on closed cliff walks
tell of rock fall, create new crannies,
where brave jackdaws attend their nest.
late primroses pose pale against the black
relying on the tide's delay.
Not denying its tenacity but knows its limitations
put down their trusting roots.
It is mid May and yet
a November night less threatening.

How did fishermen survive
or sailors lured to Trebarwith Strand
by wreckers sacrificing lives
for untaxed tobacco, brandy, lace for wives.

Who thought of making ships to rule the waves?
Surely they didn't start from here?
Surely some faraway shore
where even now tide ebbs, sun comes up
on palmy beaches, pale sands of tropical paradises
where the tide less often shows its hand.
When it does breaks all the rules
lifts tectonic plates to make
a disaster that would put this creek to shame, who
with all its swashbuckling bravado
will take no lives tonight.

In the mornings a playground for surfers.
Seal dressed, piercing the white capped rollers
to ride the seas, triumphant as Europa on her bull
their slim boards, already reduced, in the shop by the toilets
all they sell here except for postcards,
hot donuts, pastie café and the Pub
where the parrot according to Guy's story
flew out to sea and drowned.
'Who told you that?' 'The bar staff.'
Blown off course in these volatile waters?
Did he shout for help? Were his last words,
'Pretty Polly' or 'Pieces of eight,' a parrot's vocabulary
less use than the herring gull's webbed feet.

Did he have swallow ambitions,
expect to arrive on hot shores
pick his own fruit and nuts
not handed through the wire of Pub cage. .
Now the pull of the sea brings
the camcorders out to Pub's cliff car park
to record this particular high tide
that will be copied again and again
when all tonight's technology is out of date.

WEDDINGS AND FUNERALS

They're getting married these girls
I can remember being born, bright eyed
taken as read the hypocrisy of white dresses
Their involvement in the manners of their time,
nurses who have worked in maternity and hospices
standing here with rosebuds in their hair.

They are dying these women who remember
my birth day, 'Mabel's had another,'
Elsewhere Pearl Harbour dominated news.
Laid out in lightwood coffins, with sprays
of lilies, and crosses of chrysanthemums.

These girls to whom I once gave
teething rings and tiny t shirts, are asking for
duvet covers and dinner plates. My aunts
who sent me books and soap shaped
like Donald Duck are being buried
in country churchyards or incinerated among
tall memorials. Beth, Catherine, Julie and Jane
commit themselves to men and mortgages.

Elsie, Nancy, Hetty, Minnie and Charlie's Aunt
are being committed to their maker. Remaining
spouses, nieces or grandchildren go back
to sherry, ham sandwiches and reminiscences.

All those game filled Christmasses
How like our mothers we all look.
How worldly wise are the grandchildren.
How sure of themselves are the brides.

Somewhere between the champagne
promises, and the laid to rest, I stand.
Here in clothes and attitudes, chosen for
the occasions and find the occasions
impose themselves on me. Everyone
has picked their favourite hymn.
There is something to be said
for middle age. Never has the view
been quite so clear. Wedding guest or
one of the bereaved? Wavering here between,
the bouquets and the wreaths.

WESTONBIRT

This tree is almost bare
pattern of branches claws the winter air.
Only the odd yellow leaf
clue to the garland of gold
on the ground underneath.

All around, yellow, crimson, brown
these trees have thrown
their bright clothes down.
Planted to make the most of October
let themselves go.
The party's almost over.

Arriving late at the aboretum's ball
walk in November's early dark,
glad to find someone has lit a fire,
kindling rotten logs, dead wood
gives back, the warmth the season steals,
glows as other lights go out.

The Douglas Fir's discarded needles
make a rusty blanket on the ground
finds comfort like a cat
to cuddle winter sleepers.
But in the centre, green sword thrusts up
reaching for the sky,
reminding us there'll be another spring
even here where dying is such a performance

But I'm identifying with the trees.
Ideas above my station?
We are as the leaves, these
I kick aside, who won't be invited back.
They've had their spring, their sunny days,
wet weekends, soft snow
and felt the North wind that doth blow,
now the drama of the fall.
That's all.

WHITE ELEPHANT

We wake to the world redecorated
A makeover made in heaven
Everything painted, totally matching,
this cold cushioning. Every twist
of the twisted willow, fat with snow,
every bird in the neighbourhood
our feathered friend, foul weather friend,
waiting to be fed, sharing winter habitat,
not just blackbirds, blue tits, cocky robin,
but shyer species, have spread their wings
eager for our offerings.

As these flakes spread, a virus,
everyone's caught it. Not just trees,
trees are used to transformation
Dressing up in new leaves for a thousand springs
Blossomed, berried, autumn coloured,
bare branches showing off their shape,
adapt to snowy finery, accept
this season's giddiness inclusive as a plague
the fence, the car, the dustbins brook no differences.

The news is full of it, the newsreaders excited
Telling how the traffic, falters, stops, slips,
The depth of it, the accidents waiting to,
or already happened.
The docks are frozen, schools are closed.
Go careful with that grit.
Everything slows for snow, except the children,
introduced to this slippery hill, all kitted out
in Christmas gloves and anoraks.
The snow gives wheels to plastic
momentum to the slope.

Being human we build our likenesses or
make balls for weapons till, suddenly
outlined on the hill, a white elephant.

Not even looking out of place.

We photograph, record, this new environment,
Adapt though it won't last. Not here, in the south west,
an occasional visitor. Snow knows,
how quickly it can outstay its welcome.
Wonder turn to inconvenience.

Elsewhere the weather is much nastier than this,
upturns the infrastructure on a sunny island,
world's cameras swing as does our attention
snow slinks off, unnoticed in the rain.
But today, today a white elephant
makes a cold zoo on the golf.

AN OFFSIDE VIEW

Watching a programme on the history channel
about William Wilberforce
my son, blue eyed, fair skinned
middle aged according to the calendar
but autism keeps him young, looks up to say,
"White people were slaves too,"
as though wanting to be included
among this victim hood,
staining the pages of our caravan
down the long road from
cave to second home in Spain.

"Yes all nations kept slaves," I agree,
"but this was the Transatlantic Trade
which started close to home, white merchants
buying black men from West Africa
to work on the sugar plantations in America."
I stretch my secondary modern school geography
including of course long terms at the university of life.
"Rounded up by fellow Africans to be
sold down river. But Bristol Merchant Venturer's
got rich, shipping them to sell in
... people markets"
I add with emphasis, a market,
something he can understand, relate to.

"They do sell people today," he still insists.
Unimpressed somehow, having heard it all before perhaps
We live three miles from Bristol on the old milestone
That once stood opposite my junior school
Or the news, full of tribal fighting
and the crumpled cities of Syria.
The bombs of ISIS bursting erratically

on cartoonist, tube traveller, sun lounger, Paris dancer.
Maybe he doesn't differentiate
The best of cases can be overstated
lose their impact.

All it seems is war and exploitation,
aware of people trafficking.
Those who paid out, to come in,
sound similar to a literal mind
to traded people picking cotton
in a South American summer.

He watches the history channel a lot
is most shocked by Henry the VIII's
cavalier dismissal of his wives.
So many examples of
mans inhumanity to man
and all the women, scrubbing for the scrubbed.

"Well it's illegal to sell people now
they'd get put in prison."
Somehow this summing up of abolition
falls flat, fails to get across
the legacy of that dark trade
its long shadow lit up by interested parties.
"They do sell people," he insists.
"OK. Who?" I pass the ball to him.
"Mum, they sell footballers, they do."

PEAR DROP

The pears are falling again,
every October brings them down.
One by one despite the mild Autumn,
landing solid among lilac leaves,
bruising themselves on the grass.
Their time is up.

Sometimes one makes it to November,
the fittest perhaps, but not always,
the pick of the crop.
The shapeliest, bulging in all
the pear places, unblemished,
may be the first to fall.
We exclaim over this little tragedy
carry our trophy to ripen
on the kitchen window sill.
Or wrap like Jacks head in brown paper,
while the ones with the hard black patches
skagging their skin like bark,
the blotched and unevenly pear shaped
hang on to an out of reach branch
stay till the ants and the starlings
have gone right through to the core.

Those who had such a good start
blossom dropping to reveal green beginning,
promising gold skinned maturity,
on some sunny Autumn day
half a calendar away.
All the odds on their survival
lost, on the toss of a branch.

I look at my family tree
So many dates are joined up,
another one this year.

My brother who should have been here
this November, to appear
in the firework photograph
be seen in another bright flash.

A FATHERS DEATH (1979)

Another lifetime slips into past tense.
Geranium cuttings killed by the frost,
goldfish frozen into ponds.
His world has stopped.
Birds and the betting shop,
birds almost more of a gamble,
a thousand shocks, exotic birds are heir to.
Still expecting to come up on the pools,
plaintive letters from Vernons'
land posthumous on the mat.

Four children, not pushed,
but ambitious we succeed by chance.
Worried most we might upset the neighbours,
fall from local grace.
Three survive, the gap my bright blonde sister left
twenty years not closed.
Sadder still than this winter garden,
my father's raw absence, a date
that nothing cancels.

In old photographs a handsome man
in his boater and striped blazer,
grinning at antique girls on park benches.
And only yesterday broad faced, blue eyed, big smile
so many enthusiasms, ambitions not realised
though somehow less efficient than our mother.

Mr. Wilmot, who owns land round here
gets off his off his bike to say
'I was at the grammar with your father,
he could run.' I cannot share
a picture of a schoolboy running, more
the whist drive, down the Legion,
fussing over goldfish, counting hen's eggs,
a baby bird, warming by the wireless.

Though pictured still on the Cricket club wall.
part of an historic team, a tenplate of my son.
Remember warmer days, car trips to Lyme Regis.
Quiet tide rising over fossilised rocks,
limit of our childhood horizons.
At least we saw the sea.
Historical figure I most identified with,
Mary Anning. Oh to find an ichthyosaurus,
hiding so long, to be unravelled by,
the crumbing cliffs and me.

Death is so greedy today
already making faces at our mother.
My brother drives her off
to his luxury bungalow.
Its her 65th birthday tomorrow
but all the X rays say there wont be another.

In the aviary, a foreign bird
fluffs up turquoise feathers
against, an English February

TSUNAMI

From the aerial photograph
it looks like a holiday brochure
they always come out at this time of year
with the diets and double discounted sofas.
Bodies lying on the beach
privileged westerners, soaking up a foreign sun,
with umbrellas in their drinks.
Catered for by the locals,
hiring out snorkels and surfboards.
Packaging their natural advantages
making a living from visitor's playtime.
From the helicopter this looks like luxury.
The rich west? Not all the west are rich,
not all the natives are poor, but its the way to bet?

This is a long shot, closer up these aren't privileged,
they're dead. Their bodies not browning,
but swelling in the heat
unrecognisable by the parents
flying out to claim remains, only DNA or dental work
the birthday watch or particular T shirt identify.
Their global children pulled
out of hasty graves, wrapped less carefully
than the Christmas presents
never worn, or played, or taken back.

Great leveller, the big wave rushing in.
Scavenger doesn't discriminate, sucking up
whatever lies in its path, this almost unprecedented
parting of tectonic plates extending it's reach.
Mainly the indigenous, the fishing boats and surfers
Those who live by the beach, die by the beach,
those who come to holiday, explore, discover.
 'Where would you rather be?'
Asked the man on his Christmas day call
to his family in winter cold UK.
Who'll never ring home again.

The local children sent by their father
to collect the dead fish
an unexpected bounty the erratic
tide brings in. The father who didn't realize
the great wave going back was just gathering in
more of the ocean to rush forward
devour their gleaning.

The people in bungalows breakfasting on the beach
'How lucky to get one so close to the sea'
postcards made poignant already winging home.
Fair game for the tsunami
A new word in all our vocabularies
(tsu) harbour (nami) wave fr. Japan.
Explain the papers like dictionaries,
Spell check accepts.

Drowned because they were there.
Who didn't manage to avoid the passing fridge
cling on to the convenient palm tree
text back their luck and enterprise?
The day the earth moved and ran up a death toll
our calculators couldn't translate
aid agencies floundered with the enormity
of the devastation and the response.
Now they wait for body bags
as we wait for the refuse collectors
to take away the Christmas detritus.

PHEASANTS

Spring's green edge
ripples along the hawthorn hedge,
heaves itself up through old trees
along the gorge, below the bridge.

On the motorway
blooming gorse is yellower than
the daffodils, planted particularly
to join this happy bank.
Shake their heads above country cousins,
self seeded primroses, already established,
holding their ground, who once
inherited the earth
and would be most missed,
when push and shove
has settled all its differences.

Overhead, birds of prey hover.
Wait, for the motorist to provide their next meal
lay tarmac's long table.
The road to Devon is littered with dead pheasants.
Ruffled feathers and bloody entrails
meshed to make a buzzard's lunch.
Designer beak pecks at wet heart.

Beside the post box
a pheasant stands, upright, penguin smart,
red neck, new paint against
the green unwinding of an English March.
On patrol but no powers to intervene,
between, car tyre and stupid birds.

Two females flap down the steep bank.
We wait as they hesitate, then change their minds.
Wait again to see them safely across, drive on.
But looking back, watch one of them collide
with the impatient wheels of the car behind.

This spring feels ominous,
I cough but my contemporaries
are threatened with malignant tumours,
coffined with heart attacks.
New year, new gaps.

Funeral parlours become our meeting halls.
we grow adept at condolences.
The sky is overcast, masks,
the shadow of the buzzard overhead.

I stand, the bright bird watching,
but no authority to stop the traffic.

TIDELINES

The wind comes with us
despite the sun on sea lighting layered water.
Stretching over field and cliff
as England narrows, tapers down
we cross its breadth from shore to shore.
This island home, its stony borders
battered by oceans, sea birds
following their hunger, wave by wave.

As we in our holiday chalet
listen to sea's insistence
mesmerized by tides.
Crossing moors accompanied by lark song
swallow swerve, jackdaw plod,
magpie's awkward hurry, rabbits worry.
While thin gravestones remind us,
we go, this stays.

Bigger views come in on different waves.
News of rougher lives
People for whom the sea is not a holiday
But an escape route and the bar is high.
In inadequate boats they come
Those who survive the journey?
Not for everyone the relief of arrival
not for everyone the promised land,
not got it in writing, strangers on the shore
not as welcome as the swallows,
regulars, coming so far on sharp wings
to forage an English spring.

More like the gulls, 'Please don't feed..
Say the notices: Feed one, feed all.
and still they wait, sharp beak,
yellow eye, watching you eat.

"Let nature care for them."
Ah nature that fecund mother did she expect
so many children, filling vacuums,
hoovering up, upsetting the balancing act.

Birds flying in, fighting over everything
the sea brings in, seeking new pastures.
Born equal only in our common greed,
need to survive. But we're equipped
with bigger brains, less specialized,
devise new paths.

Some come running from tyranny
with no alternatives, some just seeking greener fields.
Adventurers almost or even invaders
with different agendas, are we planting
dragons teeth? Some calling in
favours from centuries back?

There are no safe harbours.
Even here where the sea
is a playground for summer surfers
the Art studios, icecream eaters.
Punters spilling from pretty Pubs.
Old ships named old wrecks explained
Wind and weather, squabbling sailors.
winter storms, hard rocks.
Not all accidents, some deliberate.
Only Jesus walked on water
even he, trod carefully.

HK/UK

Struggling in the breeze and humidity of Hong Kong
I tried to find a breeze
among orange flowered trees
I longed for England and its' bluebell woods.

Till driving home from Heathrow in the rain;
How uninviting that wet swathe
how dearly bought the hundred shades of green.
Something sinister about the bluebells
an inky stain, rain won't wash out,
rain encourages.

Missing the thin shade, of orange flowered trees,
the turquoise harbour where no breeze
disturbed the waves, swallows nesting against
a pagoda's yellow glaze.

Here they return to the Angel, fly in
to what used to be stables,
now labelled Ladies and Gents
and in their rafters make
mud nests, but not a summer.